Claymation Sensation

SPACE CLAYMATION

Emily Reid

Published in 2017 by **Windmill Books**,
an Imprint of Rosen Publishing
29 East 21st Street, New York, NY 10010

Produced for Rosen by BlueAppleWorks Inc.

Creative Director: Melissa McClellan
Managing Editor for BlueAppleWorks: Melissa McClellan
Design: T.J. Choleva
Editor: Kelly Spence
Puppet Artisans: Janet Kompare-Fritz (p. 14, 16, 18); Jane Yates (p. 10, 12, 20, 22)

Picture credits: Plasticine letters:Vitaly Korovin/Shutterstock; title page, TOC, Austen Photography; p. 4 Sony Pictures
Releasing/Photofest; p.5 Janet Kompare-Fritz; ; p. 6 left to right and top to bottom: ukrfidget/Shutterstock; Andrey Eremin/
Shutterstock; exopixel /Shutterstock; Lukas Gojda/Shutterstock; koosen/Shutterstock; Irina Nartova/Shutterstock; STILLFX/
Shutterstock; Picsfive/Shutterstock; Charles0890/Shutterstock; Darryl Brooks/Shutterstock; Winai Tepsuttinun/Shutterstock;
Pelham James Mitchinson/Shutterstock; Yulia elf_inc Tropina/Shutterstock; Austen Photography; All For You /Shutterstock;
Radu Bercan/Shutterstock; Igor Kovalchuk/Shutterstock; Austen Photography; p. 7 left to right and top to bottom: Ilike/
Shutterstock; Tarzhanova/Shutterstock; Austen Photography; kamomeen /Shutterstock; Lesha/Shutterstock; ikurdyumov/
Shutterstock; Austen Photography; Ilike/Shutterstock; p-8 to 27 Austen Photography; p. 28 left Valentina Razumova/
Shutterstock; p. 29 upper left Warongdech/Shutterstock;p. 29 top right Anneka/Shutterstock; p. 29 right taelove7/
Shutterstock; p. 30, 31 Austen Photography

Cataloging-in-Publication Data

Names: Reid, Emily.
Title: Space claymation / Emily Reid.
Description: New York : Windmill Books, 2017. | Series: Claymation sensation | Includes index.
Identifiers: ISBN 9781499481006 (pbk.) | ISBN 9781499481020 (library bound) | ISBN 9781499481013 (6 pack)
Subjects: LCSH: Animation (Cinematography)--Juvenile literature. | Sculpture--Technique--Juvenile literature.|
    Space (Art)--Juvenile literature.
Classification: LCC TR897.5 R45 2017 | DDC 777'.7--dc23

Manufactured in the United States of America
CPSIA Compliance Information: Batch #BS16PK: For Further Information contact Rosen Publishing, New York, New York at 1-800-237-9932

Contents

What Is Claymation?

It's time to blast off on an out-of-this-world Claymation adventure! Claymation, also known as clay **animation**, combines **stop-motion** animation with characters or puppets made out of modeling clay to create movies or short videos.

Stop-motion animation creates the illusion of movement when a series of still images, called **frames**, are quickly played in sequence. Each frame shows a slight change in position from the previous frame. Clay characters are easy to move and reposition to show these actions in small steps. The smaller the movements, the smoother the sequence appears. It takes several frames to make a Claymation movie. Animations can be created using many devices, including a traditional camera, smartphone, or tablet.

Full-length Claymation movies take months and lots of money to make. Often the latest technology is involved. In The Pirates! Band of Misfits, released in 3-D in 2012, some backgrounds were digitally created using a green screen.

Claymation Tip

There are lots of apps you can use to create your Claymation movie. These apps let you shoot and edit your movie using one device. Make sure to ask permission before you download any apps to your smartphone, tablet, or computer.

All types of filmmaking, including Claymation, tell a story. To start, brainstorm an idea for your space adventure. Think of a beginning, middle, and end. Write a short summary of the story. How many characters do you need to tell your story? What kind of background and props will you use?

When you make a Claymation movie, it is important to map out the character's movements before you start shooting. A **storyboard** is a series of drawings that show each step of the story. Use a storyboard to figure out what actions are needed, and in what order, to tell your story from start to finish. Sketch out each scene and label it with the scene number. After the storyboard is ready, it's time to create your puppets.

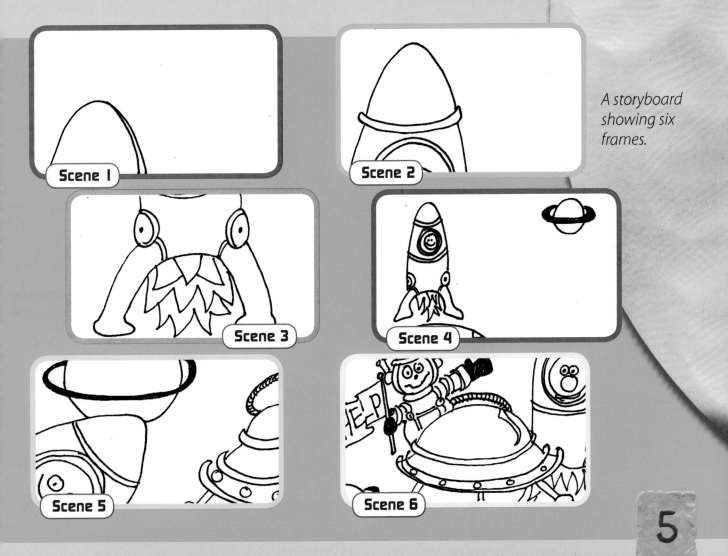

A storyboard showing six frames.

Scene 1

Scene 2

Scene 3

Scene 4

Scene 5

Scene 6

Materials and Techniques

Claymation puppets are created with nondrying, oil-based clay. Plasticine is a popular brand, although any nondrying modeling clay will do. This type of clay is moldable enough to create a character, flexible enough to allow that character to move in many ways, and dense enough to hold its shape when combined with a wire **armature**.

Materials That You Will Need

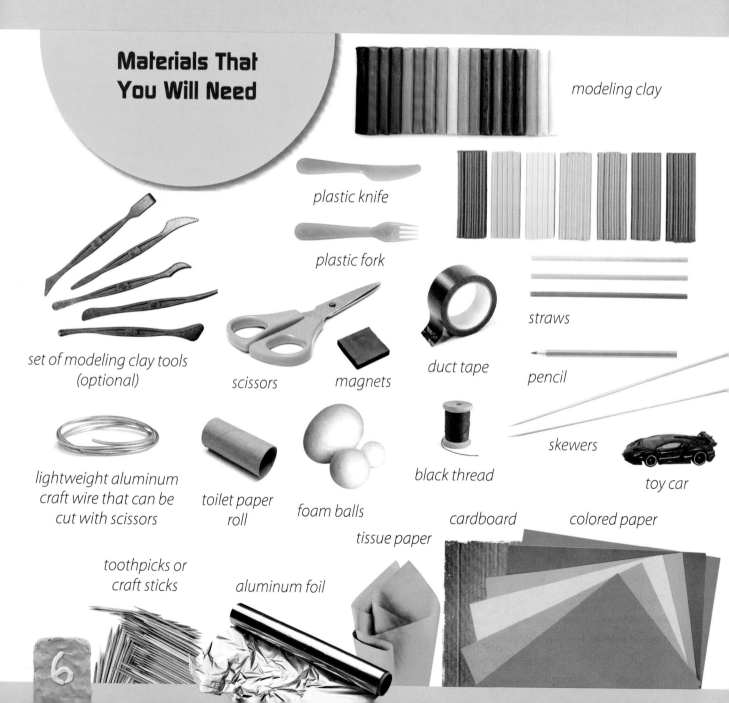

modeling clay

plastic knife

plastic fork

set of modeling clay tools (optional)

scissors

magnets

duct tape

straws

pencil

skewers

toy car

lightweight aluminum craft wire that can be cut with scissors

toilet paper roll

foam balls

black thread

cardboard

colored paper

tissue paper

toothpicks or craft sticks

aluminum foil

Working with Clay

Modeling clay is oily and can be messy to work with. Prepare a work area. A piece of cardboard or foam board is great to work on. Wash your hands well when you finish working, as they will be oily, too.

Basic Shapes

All of these shapes can be made big or small or thin or thick, depending on the amount of clay used and the pressure applied. Use your fingers to squish, smooth, pinch, flatten, and poke the clay into whatever shape you want.

To form a ball, move your hands in a circle while pressing the clay lightly between them.

To create a pancake shape, roll a ball and flatten it between your thumb and fingers. Smooth the edges if they crack.

To make a snake shape, roll the clay on a flat surface with your fingers.

To form a teardrop, pinch and roll one end of a ball into a point.

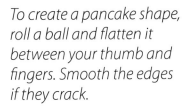

To create a cylinder, roll a large piece of clay in your hand, then roll it on a flat surface to smooth. Press each end into the table to flatten it.

To make a slab, start with a large piece and flatten it on your work surface. Keep pressing the clay out and away from the center until it is as flat as you want it.

Modeling Tips

● Always start by kneading the clay in your hands to warm it up and soften it.

● You can mix different colors together to create new colors. Just squish the clay in your hands until it is blended completely or leave it partially blended to create a marble effect.

● Make your puppets about the same size as an action figure, between 4 and 6 inches (10 and 15 cm) tall. They should be big enough to move around but not so big they fall over.

Body Parts and Armatures

Puppets can be made in many ways. The simple ones require only modeling clay and some patience. If you decide to create more complicated puppets, you will need additional elements to give the puppets structure and support, such as wire armatures and foam shapes. It is a good idea to keep anything that is on top of the puppet light so it does not droop during animation. Using a lightweight foam ball should do the trick.

1 Get different size foam shapes from a local craft or dollar store.

2 Carefully cover the foam with a thin layer of clay.

3 Smooth any bumps with your fingers until you have an even surface.

4 Attach the puppet's legs and arms to the finished head. Make sure that your puppet can stand up on its own. You are ready to roll!

Claymation Tip

Use foam shapes to create bulky body parts. This makes your puppets lighter and reduces the amount of clay that you will need to create puppets.

Stability

Make sure your character has a big enough base or feet to support its weight. If necessary, you can stabilize it with putty or put pushpins through the puppet's feet to hold it in place.

Armatures

Armatures function as a skeleton that holds the puppet parts together and allows for them to move easily. Wire-based armatures are made using strands of lightweight wire. Whenever useful, you can combine an armature with foam pieces to create a base for your puppet. Make sure you don't make the clay too thick around the armature, or your puppet will be difficult to move.

Be creative with the details. Try new things. Use aluminum foil to add futuristic touches to some puppets. Have fun with it!

To make an armature for a figure start with a long piece of wire. Fold it in half. Twist the wire to form a loop at the top.

Take one piece of the wire and bend it to form one of the figure's arms. You can make it whatever length you choose. At the end of the arm, loop the wire and twist it back on itself. Repeat this step on the opposite side using the other length of wire.

Twist both wires together to form the body.

Make the legs and feet following the same steps used for the arms. If you have extra wire left, cut it off or wind it around the body.

You can make your astronaut puppet lighter by using a foam ball for its middle.

9

Planets

The sun lies at the center of our solar system. There are eight planets that orbit this enormous star. Moving away from the sun, the planets are Mercury, Venus, Earth, Mars, Jupiter, Saturn, Uranus, and Neptune. Each planet in our solar system is unique. Earth is the only place known to support life. Mars is nicknamed the red planet. Saturn is surrounded by icy rings.

Earth

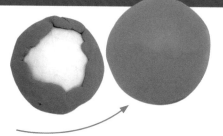

1 *Use a lightweight foam ball for the base to make the puppet lighter. Roll a thin slab of blue clay to cover the ball. To smooth the edges, roll the ball in between your hands.*

2 *Press out two thin slabs of green clay. With a globe as a guide, use the plastic knife to cut the slabs into the shapes of the continents. Press the cutouts onto the blue ball.*

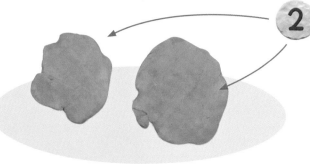

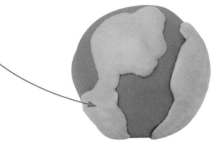

Mars

1 *Twist together strands of red and orange clay. Smooth the clay so the colors blend slightly.*

2 *Press the blended clay into a thin slab, then cover a foam ball. Roll out some snakes and other shapes and press them onto the ball.*

Saturn

1 Roll several snakes using different shades of yellow and orange clay. Twist the snakes so the colors blend together. Use the clay to make a large pancake, then cover a foam ball.

2 For Saturn's rings, roll two snakes using yellow and orange clay. Join the ends of each snake together to make a circle. Press the two circles together, then flatten to form the rings.

3 Push craft sticks into the middle of the foam to form a circle. Place the flattened rings on top. Make sure the craft sticks are fully covered by the clay.

Claymation Tip

Tie a long piece of black thread around each planet. Smooth the clay over the string to hide it. Leave a long piece to attach the planets to the set (see page 26). When shooting your movie, you can make your planets orbit around the sun or simply float in the background. You can also make more planets to create a film about the entire solar system.

Alien Puppet

Aliens are life-forms from a planet other than Earth. No proof of alien life has been found, but many scientists believe that extraterrestrial beings exist. Until proof is found, aliens exist only in our imaginations. They are often portrayed as little green men in stories, TV shows, and movies.

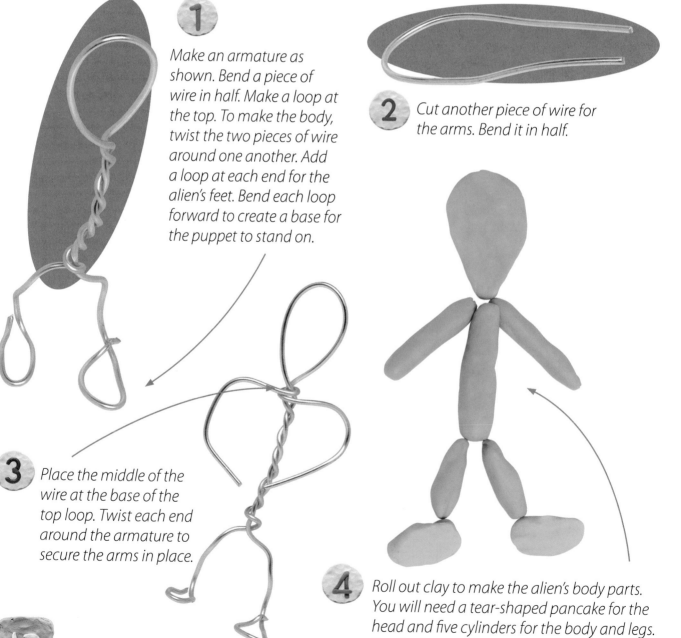

1 *Make an armature as shown. Bend a piece of wire in half. Make a loop at the top. To make the body, twist the two pieces of wire around one another. Add a loop at each end for the alien's feet. Bend each loop forward to create a base for the puppet to stand on.*

2 *Cut another piece of wire for the arms. Bend it in half.*

3 *Place the middle of the wire at the base of the top loop. Twist each end around the armature to secure the arms in place.*

4 *Roll out clay to make the alien's body parts. You will need a tear-shaped pancake for the head and five cylinders for the body and legs. For the feet, make two oval pancakes.*

5 Press the pieces of clay onto the armature. Add more clay where needed to cover the wire. Smooth any seams with your fingers.

6 Gently press the wire feet into the clay feet. Fold the clay around the armature. Add extra clay if needed to fully cover the wire.

7 For the eyes, make two flat oval shapes with pointed ends. Roll two small black snakes, flatten, and press into the eyes. Press the eyes onto the alien's face. For the nose, make a small oval with pointed ends. Flatten the nose and place it under the eyes. Use a flattened snake to decorate the alien's body.

8 Form hands by pinching the clay at the end of each arm into two fingers with pointed ends. Use a modeling tool to carve toes on the feet.

Claymation Tip

When animating your alien, its arms and legs can both move. Smooth any creases that form after positioning the arms or legs.

UFO

A UFO is an unidentified flying object. It is something that is seen in the sky but cannot be identified. Often reported UFOs can be explained. The ones that cannot be remain a mystery. UFOs are also known as flying saucers. Some people believe UFOs are spaceships carrying alien life.

1 Draw a saucer shape on a piece of cardboard, then cut it out.

2 Scrunch up two pieces of foil. Make sure the balls are smaller than the cardboard. The first ball should also be slightly larger than the second. Use tape to attach the smaller ball to the middle of the saucer.

Build the Bottom Part

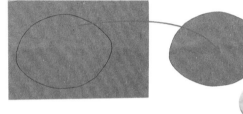

 3 Press out a large, thin pancake shape. It needs to be bigger than the cardboard. Use a different color to make a smaller pancake. Press the smaller pancake into the center of the larger pancake.

4 Lay the pancake over the top of the cardboard. The foil will form a bump in the middle. Fold the extra clay under the edge of the saucer.

5 To make the UFO's legs, cut three short pieces of straw and three slightly longer pieces of wire. Roll six small balls of clay. Insert a piece of wire into a straw, then push one end of the straw into a ball. Press the other end into the bottom of the UFO. Repeat this step to make two more legs.

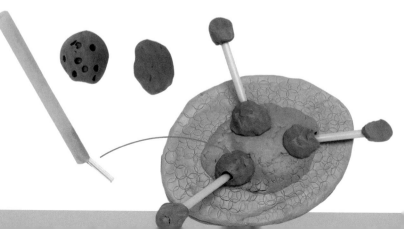

Build the Top Part

6

Flip the saucer over. Use a green pancake to cover the top. Next, place the larger foil ball in the middle. Form a thin pancake that is larger than the foil. Lay it over the ball to form a bump. Press down along the outer edge to join the top and bottom layers.

7

Use the plastic knife to carefully cut a small foam ball in half. Cover the ball with foil. Attach the ball to the top of the saucer using wire or a toothpick.

8

Roll three snakes using different colors. Press them around the outer edge, the inner circle, and the foil ball. Make squiggly lines in the clay for decoration.

9

Press beads into small balls of clay, then place the balls around the UFO's outer edge. Add a white snake to the top of the foil ball.

Claymation Tip

You can create a dramatic scene showing your alien beaming up into the UFO. See page 28 for an out-of-this-world lighting technique to help stage the scene.

Spaceship

Apollo 11 was the first manned spaceship to land on the moon. It touched down on July 20, 1969. American astronaut Neil Armstrong was on board. When he stepped onto the moon's surface, he said the famous words, "One small step for [a] man, one giant leap for mankind."

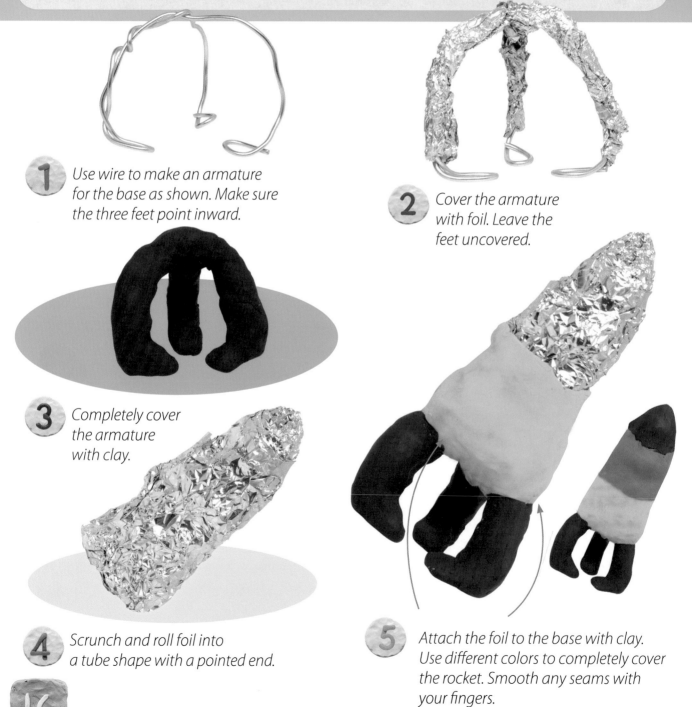

1 *Use wire to make an armature for the base as shown. Make sure the three feet point inward.*

2 *Cover the armature with foil. Leave the feet uncovered.*

3 *Completely cover the armature with clay.*

4 *Scrunch and roll foil into a tube shape with a pointed end.*

5 *Attach the foil to the base with clay. Use different colors to completely cover the rocket. Smooth any seams with your fingers.*

6 Roll five snake shapes using yellow clay. Flatten the snakes, then press one along each seam where the different colors join.

7 Press out thin slabs using red, yellow, and orange clay. With scissors, cut the slabs into flames. Press the flames together and then attach them to the bottom of the rocket.

8 For buttons, make three flat pancake shapes. Use a straw to punch a hole in the center of each circle. Place one button above each leg of the rocket.

9 Optional: Make a window with an astronaut peering out. For the window, wrap a thin snake around a white oval pancake. Use flattened pancake shapes to form a face.

Claymation Tip
When animating the rocket, it can be taking off from a planet or blasting through space.

Astronaut Puppet

An astronaut is a person who is trained to travel into space. The word "astronaut" comes from the Greek words meaning "star" and "sailor." In 1961, Russia's Yuri Gagarin became the first person to journey into space. Since then, over 520 people have made the trip.

1 *Make an armature out of wire (see page 9). Use the plastic knife to cut a foam ball in half. Attach the ball to the armature with tape.*

2 *Soften a large ball of clay. Use the clay to cover the armature. Leave the top loop, hands, and feet uncovered.*

3 *Use brown or beige clay to form a small pancake. This will be the astronaut's face. Press the face onto a small foam ball. Cover the rest of the ball with yellow clay. Add two flat pancakes on top for the helmet. Gently press the head onto the top loop of the armature.*

5 *Roll several snake shapes. Coil the snakes around the arms, legs, and neck to make the astronaut's spacesuit. For the shoulders, wrap a wide snake around the top of each arm.*

4 *For the boots, roll four ovals. Flatten two ovals and place them under the feet. Press the wire into them, then press another oval on top. Smooth the edges. Form two gloves using extra clay. Attach one glove to the end of each arm.*

6 Flatten two white balls for eyes, then add two tiny black balls for pupils. Press the eyes together and add them to face. Make a nose from a small ball. Use a modeling tool to carve the astronaut's mouth.

7 Roll a small ball, then cut it in half. Roll four tiny balls. Cut four small pieces of wire. Push each wire into a tiny ball. Stick two wires into the top of each half ball. Press one half ball onto each side of the head. Cut a small rectangle of aluminum foil. Press it onto the astronaut's stomach and outline it with snake shapes.

8 For the astronaut's backpack, make a clay rectangle. Place two tiny balls and a small square of foil on the front. Cut the bendable part of a straw and form a loop on the top of the backpack. Roll and flatten three snakes. Press two snakes into the top of the back to form straps. Press the backpack into the back of the puppet. Then, attach the other end of the straps to the astronaut's front. Use the last snake to join the two straps. Add two flattened balls as buttons.

Claymation Tip

When animating the puppet, the astronaut can moonwalk across the set. What will your astronaut discover on his or her space adventure?

19

Space Rover

A space rover is a robotic vehicle that is sent to explore the surface of a distant planet. It is designed to drive over very rough terrain. The rover collects data and sends it back to scientists on Earth.

 For this puppet, you will need an old toy car (or you can buy one in a dollar store). Cover the car with clay. Leave the wheels uncovered and make sure they can still spin.

 Blend together two colors to create a marbled effect. Roll out four cylinders. To make treads, flatten each cylinder. Use the plastic knife or modeling tool to make shallow cuts along each slab as shown.

 Make eight flat pancake shapes. Make shallow cuts in a circular pattern. Press a flattened ball into the center of each circle.

 To make the wheels, use the plastic knife to carefully cut the ends off of four small foam balls. Wrap a tread around each ball. Press a pancake shape onto each end.

 Cut two pieces of wire that are wide enough to lay across the car. Use the wire as an axle to join two wheels together. Repeat this step for the other two wheels. Place one wire across the front of the car. Place the second across the back. The rover's wheels should sit just above the car's wheels.

20

6 Cut the sides and bottom away from a foam ball to create a half moon shape. Cover the foam in clay. This will be the rover's body. Place it on top of the car, covering the wires. Roll a snake shape, then wrap it around the body to hide the seam.

7 Make instruments for the rover. Cover wire or craft sticks with clay. Add balls or pancakes to one end. Attach the other end to the rover. Make another instrument out of a bendable straw. Pack clay into one end of the straw, then push in a craft stick. Cover the straw and stick the instrument into the rover.

8 Use two small rectangular slabs to make two solar panels. Add lines with a toothpick. Wrap a thin snake around the slab and press it onto the rover's body.

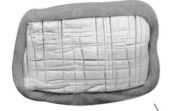

9 Decorate the rover with thin snakes. Wrap them around the instruments or press them onto the different parts of the rover.

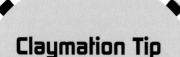

Claymation Tip

When animating your rover, it can roll along the planet's surface. The instruments can also be positioned to conduct experiments and collect data.

21

Space Shuttle

The space shuttle was a manned spacecraft that was launched like a rocket into space. When its mission was complete, the shuttle touched down on a runway. It was the first spacecraft to make a return trip from space. The shuttle was used to conduct experiments, transport satellites into space, and carry astronauts to the space station. It flew its final mission in 2011.

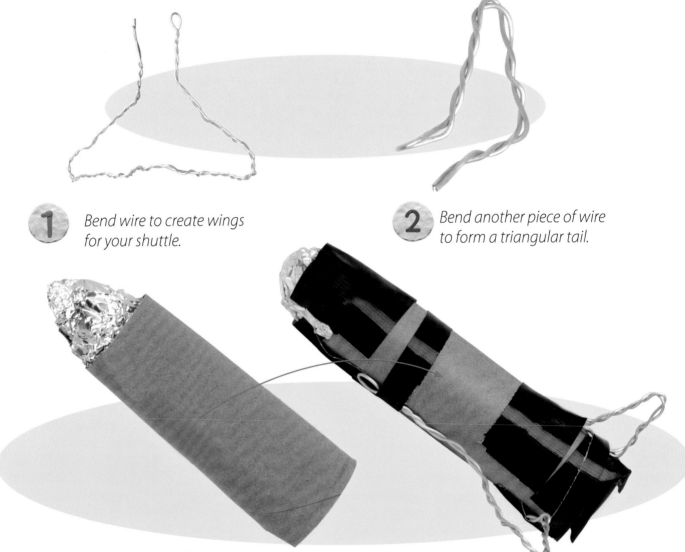

1 Bend wire to create wings for your shuttle.

2 Bend another piece of wire to form a triangular tail.

3 Stuff a toilet paper roll with crumpled up paper. Use foil to make a small cone. Place the cone inside the roll as shown.

4 Tape the wire pieces to the roll. Use extra tape to attach the cone and to close up the open end.

6 Make a windshield shape from a thin slab of clay. Outline it with snake shapes. Press it on above the nose of the shuttle.

5 Roll several thin slabs of clay. Use the slabs to completely cover the armature.

7 Use different colors to make several thin snakes. Use them to add details to the shuttle.

Claymation Tip

When animating the puppet, you can make it fly through the solar system. You can also add landing gear following the same steps used for the rover. Then your shuttle can touch down or take off on a runway.

The Props

Props are used in the creation of the movie. They decorate the set. Props add visual interest to the movie. Sometimes the puppets interact with them. In a space Claymation, the props can be anything you would see flying through space or exploring the moon or a distant planet. Use your imagination!

 To make a meteor, blend several colors of clay together, then roll the ball into a large slab. Use a knife to cut a circular top with a fiery tail trailing behind. You can attach the meteor to the background of the set. If you want to animate it, use wire to give the tail extra support.

2 *Make panels for a satellite by pressing out two thin rectangular slabs. Push two short pieces of wire into the slabs as shown. Add three thin white snakes. Use a knife to carefully cut three foam balls in half. Stack the balls on top of one another. Push a small piece of wire through the middle to join them. Cover and decorate the stack with clay. Insert the visible wire into each side of the foam to join the satellite's panels to its body.*

Use clay to make a rocky moon surface for the astronaut to explore. Mix together several dark colors of clay. Squish the clay into an uneven slab. Use a modeling tool or pencil to add more texture.

 Make a two-dimensional planet to float in the background. Blend together several colors of clay, then press out a pancake shape. Roll some snakes and press them onto the front of the pancake.

5 Use white or bright yellow clay to make stars. To make a star, roll a small ball. Flatten the ball and pinch out five points. When you are ready to film, stick the stars onto the background of the set. You can make the stars appear to twinkle by removing them for one shot then putting them back for the next.

 Make a rocky planet surface by crumpling up tissue paper.

Claymation Tip

Use two magnets to animate your meteor. Press one magnet into the back of the meteor. When you're ready to begin, place the meteor on the front of the background. Match the other magnet on the back. The meteor can now slowly blaze across the sky in your movie. You can also use this technique to animate your two-dimensional planet.

The Set

The set is where you will film your movie. It is the landscape in which your story will come to life. A set can be as simple as a piece of paper taped to the wall or more complex. The set needs to be large enough for your puppets to be able to move around.

Basic Set

The most basic set is a single piece of paper or poster board. Tape one end of the paper to the wall. Pull the paper and tape the other end to the table. Leave a bit of a curve in the paper.

 You can build a simple set using a cardboard box. Use scissors to remove the flaps and one side.

2 *Tape or glue black construction paper or poster board to the inside of the box.*

3 *Use tape to join two wooden sticks together. Chopsticks work well.*

4 *Lay the stick across the top of the box. If needed, cut two notches in the cardboard to help the stick stay in place. Use black thread to hang your planets and other creations from the stick. You can slowly slide the stick along in each shot to create the illusion of movement.*

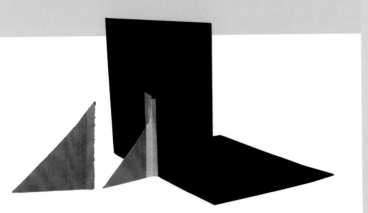

 5 You can also make a set from black foam board. Take a large piece of board and bend it in half. You can also tape together two pieces of foam board for a larger set.

Make a semicircle out of colored paper to show a planet rising in the foreground. Glue or tape to the paper at the bottom of the set.

Cut circles out of colored paper to represent distant planets.

 6 Use cardboard to make a triangle. Tape the triangle to the back of one rectangle. Bend the other rectangle to form an L shape as shown.

Alternative Set

You can paint a background directly on the cardboard. You can sprinkle salt or glitter on the paint as it dries to create a sky full of sparkling stars.

 7 Arrange your props. Before you start shooting, secure the set to the surface you are working on with tape.

Lights, Camera, . . .

To light your set, a couple of desk lamps or the overhead lights should do the trick. Don't place your set near a window or shoot outside unless it is an overcast day. Changes in lighting will cause flickering in your movie.

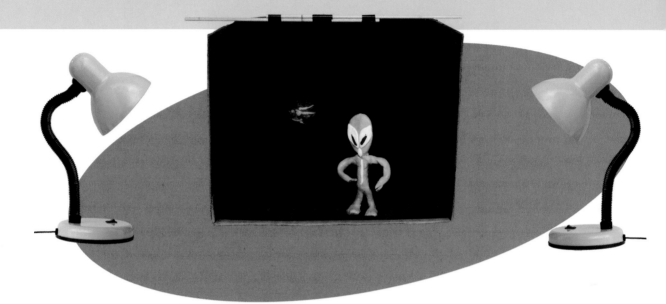

Experiment with the placement of the lamps. Take test shots to see how it looks.

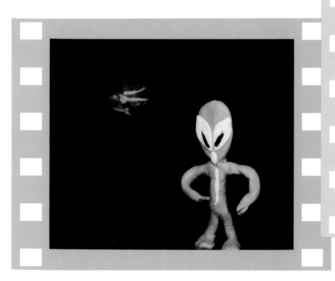

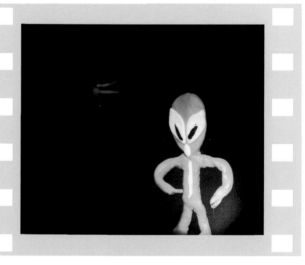

Flat, even light is created when two lamps are placed an equal distance apart. There are little or no shadows.

You can use the spotlight as part of your story to beam the alien up to the UFO.

Claymation does not require a video camera. A digital camera, smartphone camera, or tablet camera will work. Think about the camera angles you want to use while shooting your film. The angle and distance from which you capture your scene can bring your movie to life.

In a straight-on shot, the camera is lined up directly with the puppet.

Shooting the movie from above makes the puppet appear small.

A closeup shot taken from a low angle can create a dramatic effect.

. . . . Action!
Making Your Movie

It's time to make your Claymation movie! You have your storyboard, your puppet(s), your set, lights, and camera. Position the puppets on the set when you are ready to begin. Using your storyboard as a guide, start taking photos. Make sure you move your puppets in very tiny increments. The smaller the movements, the smoother the film will be. Be careful not to move the camera while taking a sequence of shots.

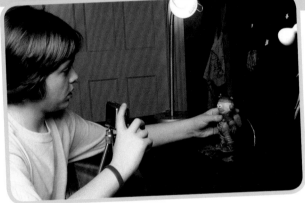

You can use a camera on a tripod and import your stills later into an animation program. Or you can use your smartphone or tablet camera to capture photos directly in a stop-motion animation app.

Make sure your hands are out of the frame after moving the puppet before taking the next shot.

It takes a lot of patience to make a Claymation film. Slowly move your puppet toward an object on your set to make it appear as if the puppet is moving on its own. If the puppet moves too far in each shot it will appear to jump rather than move in one fluid motion.

Now it's time to finish your movie. **Postproduction** is the last step in creating your Claymation film. Within your app or animation program you can edit your frames, removing any that don't work. This is also the time to add music or sound effects. Music can set the mood of the film. Different types of music can sound happy, sad, or suspenseful. There are all kinds of free sound effects on the Internet, or you can record your own. Adding effects to your movie will bring the action to life.

Finally, it's showtime! Stage a screening to share your space adventure with an audience. At the end, take a bow!

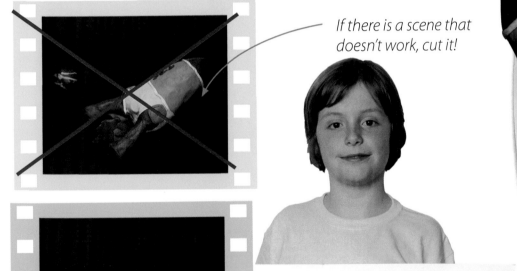

If there is a scene that doesn't work, cut it!

Use clay letters to make credits for your movie. Include a title and end credits, listing yourself and anyone else who helped.

GLOSSARY

animation In film, creating the illusion of movement using still images played in a rapid sequence.

armature A wire frame that acts as a skeleton for a sculpture made with modeling clay.

frame An individual picture in a series of images.

postproduction The final stages of finishing a movie after it has been recorded that usually involves editing and adding sound.

stop-motion An animation technique that uses a series of shots showing small movements to make characters or objects appear to move.

storyboard A series of pictures that show the scenes in an animation.

FOR MORE INFORMATION

FURTHER READING

Cassidy, John, and Nicholas Berger. *The Klutz Book of Animation.*
Palo Alto, CA: Klutz, 2010.

Grabham, Tim. *Movie Maker: The Ultimate Guide to Making Films.*
Somerville, MA: Candlewick, 2010.

Piercy, Helen. *Animation Studio.*
Somerville, MA: Candlewick, 2013.

WEBSITES

For web resources related to the subject of this book, go to:
www.windmillbooks.com/weblinks and select this book's title.

INDEX